Jurassic Brunch

Written and Illustrated
by Seth Harris

Under a starry sky, a young dinosaur named Benedict dreamt of something amazing. In his slumbering mind, he saw a fried egg, a slice of bacon, and a zesty sauce on a toasted english muffin. He saw the world's greatest breakfast sandwich.

He decided to make his dream a reality.
He composed a list ingredients.

After foraging all day, he checked his list and found that there was only one more thing to get: an egg.

I should tell you that Benedict is a very young dinosaur. He had not yet learned that you should always leave wild eggs where they lie.

Now Benedict had everything that he needed. He fried the bacon, and was about to crack the egg open when something very unexpected happened....

A pterodactyl flew out of Benedict's egg! He was very confused. It was too late in the day to go foraging again so he ate the eggless sandwich anyway.

He thought a good night's sleep would cure him of his desires, but all he dreamt about was his tasty sandwich.

The next morning,
Benedict decided to get
another egg from a
different source.

He began to feel bad about
taking the egg, but he couldn't
explain why.

As he prepared to cook breakfast, he saw the egg roll around on the ground and crack open to reveal another little dinosaur.

Benedict went to the nest where
he found the egg to put the little
dinosaur back.

But little dinosaur's family was nowhere to
be found.

The little dinosaur was all alone and scared, so he began to cry.

Little did he know, that he was beginning to attract the attention of something not-so-little.

Suddenly he saw a scary dimetrodon in the moonlight.
The dimetrodon licked his lips and began to chase after him! The little
dinosaur knew he had to run. Otherwise, he would become dinner.

He hid in a nearby bush but he knew it was only a matter of time before the dimetrodon found him.

Then the little hatchling heard a rumbling in the distance.

It was Benedict!

"Are you hungry?"
He asked.

Benedict realized that the little guy needed to learn how to protect himself. He taught him how to romp, stomp, and roar. That day Benedict decided to name him Waffles.

Benedict taught Waffles how to stalk prey without being seen. They practiced by hunting a tasty boar rat.

The baby pterodactyl would fly in and visit at least three times a day. Benedict realized that she also did not have a name, so he named her Florentine. Benedict really liked Florentine and Waffles, though they were very different from him.

Benedict was like Waffles' big brother. He even took Waffles
to his favorite place in the whole world: the firefly meadow.

Benedict had almost completely forgotten about the
bacon, egg, and cheese sandwich.

In fact, a delightful brunch could not have been further from his mind. Until one day, when they were off hunting...

Benedict saw the biggest eggs that
he had ever seen in his life.

But that egg was also not
his to take.

Don't worry, our friends got out okay.

But Benedict began to reconsider egg stealing.

Benedict decided that his egg sandwich quest was not worth it. He didn't want to steal and he didn't want to risk his life or Waffles'. So he gave up that dream.

In the morning, Waffles woke him up with a stack of biscuits.

Waffles looked like he was up to something.

Then something fell out of the sky and landed
in Benedict's frying pan.

It was an egg! and another egg! and
another!

Florentine brought
the eggs!

Benedict cooked the eggs while Waffles and Florentine played around.

That day, they had the first brunch in the history of the world.

And Benedict learned that you don't need to steal to realize your dreams. Some dreams just have a way of coming true by themselves.

-The End-

www.ingramcontent.com/pod-product-compliance
Lightning Source LLC
Chambersburg PA
CBHW060807290526
45792CB00005BA/1555